Rookie
Read-About®
Geography

MAP KEYS

D1025759

by Rebecca Olien

Content Consultant
Laura McCormick
Cartographer
XNR Productions Inc.

Children's Press®
An Imprint of Scholastic Inc.
New York Toronto London Auckland Sydney
Mexico City New Delhi Hong Kong
Danbury, Connecticut

Library of Congress Cataloging-in-Publication Data
Olien, Rebecca.
  Map keys/by Rebecca Olien.
      p. cm.—(Rookie read-about geography)
  Includes bibliographical references and index.
  ISBN-13: 978-0-531-28965-5 (lib. bdg.)   ISBN-13: 978-0-531-29289-1 (pbk.)
  1. Map reading—Juvenile literature. 2. Maps—Symbols—Juvenile
literature. I. Title.
  GA130.O55 2012
  912.01'48—dc23   2012000499

7 8 9 10 R 22 21 20 19 18 17 16

Photographs © 2013: Alamy Images/Ron Buskirk: 20; PhotoEdit/David Young-Wolff: 28;
Scholastic, Inc.: 24, 29 bottom right; Shutterstock, Inc.: 4 (iofoto), cover (maraga);
The Image Works/Jorn Stjerneklar/Impact/HIP: 26.

Maps by XNR Productions, Inc.

Table of Contents

Reading a Map

People use maps to find where to go. How do people read maps?

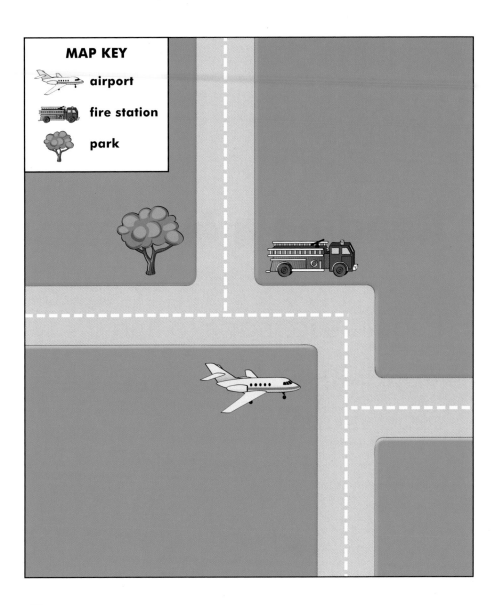

MAP KEY

airport

fire station

park

Map keys help people to read maps. A map key is in a box on the map. Can you find the map key on this town map?

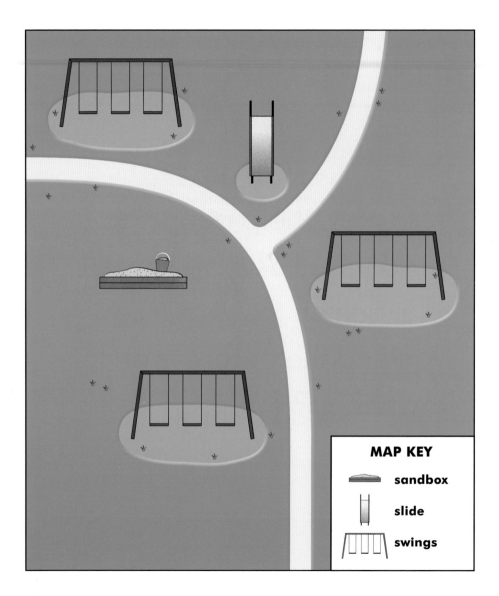

MAP KEY

sandbox

slide

swings

8

This is a map of a playground. Can you find the map key on this map?

MAP KEY

 **bird house**

 **giraffe house**

 **polar bear pool**

 reptile house

Pictures and Shapes

Sometimes maps have small pictures. The map key tells what the pictures mean.

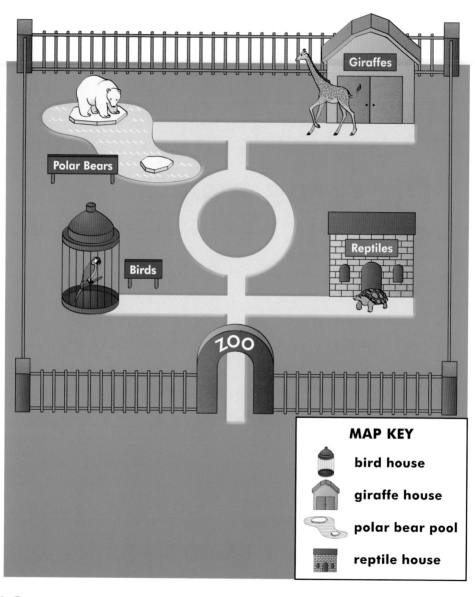

12

This is a zoo map. The map has a picture for each animal's home. Can you see the bird house on the map key?

MAP KEY

 campfire

 picnic table

 pool

 tent

Some maps have shapes. Map keys show what the shapes mean. Look at this map key. Which shape is for the tent?

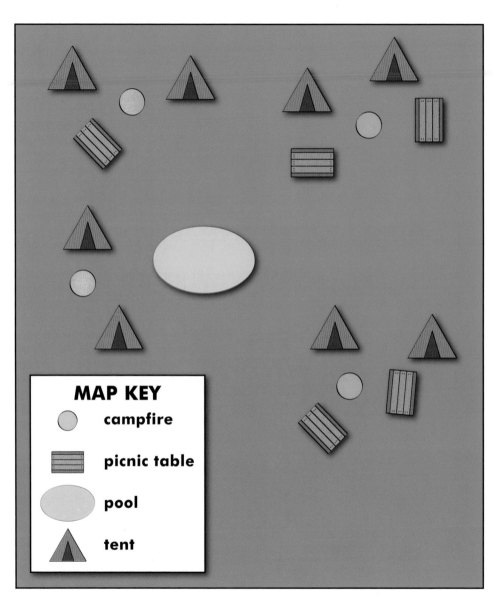

This is a map of a campground. Can you find the campfires? Can you count the picnic tables on the map?

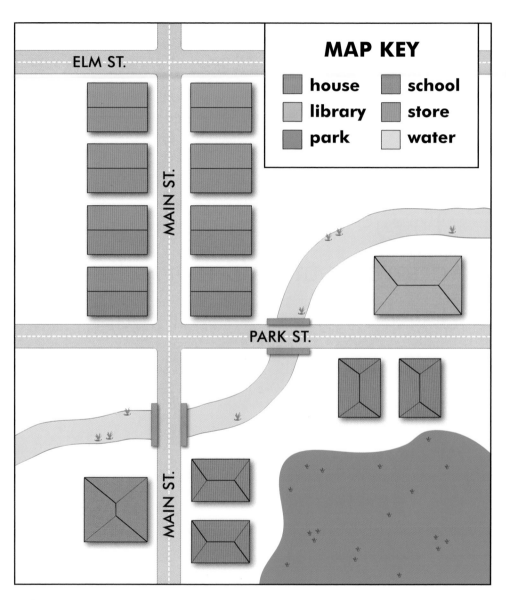

ELM ST.

MAIN ST.

MAP KEY

- house
- library
- park
- school
- store
- water

PARK ST.

MAIN ST.

18

Colors and Lines

Maps use colors. A map key shows what each color means. Which color is for the park? Can you find the park on this map?

Marjorie Harris Carr
Cross Florida Greenway

MARSHALL
SWAMP TRAIL

SE 64TH AVE
ROAD
TRAILHEAD

0   11

TEAK WAY
DRIVE
TRAILHEAD

MAP KEY:

SHIP CANAL TRAIL
1 MILE

GOPHER TRACK LOOP
1.5 MILE

MEADOWLARK LOOP
1.5 MILE

RED OAK MILE
1 MILE

8

BANYAN
ROAD
TRAILHEAD

PECAN
PASS
TRAILHEAD

5

PECAN
COURSE
CIRCLE
TRAILHEAD

4

3

2

1

BASELINE ROAD

BASELINE
ROAD
TRAILHEAD

MARICAMP ROAD

GREENWAYS & TRAILS
CONNECTING FLORIDA'S COMMUNITIES

20

Maps sometimes have lines. The lines show ways to go from place to place. Look at the map key to find the Red Oak Mile path.

NEW YORK

Allegheny Forest

PENNSYLVANIA

Pittsburgh Airport

Harrisburg

N.J.

MARYLAND

W.VA.

VIRGINIA

MAP KEY

airport

capital city

forest

road

water

All Kinds of Maps

A state map uses colors, lines, and pictures. Where is the airport? Can you find the forest?

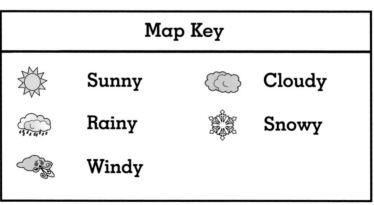

Map Key

☀	**Sunny**	☁	**Cloudy**
🌧	**Rainy**	❄	**Snowy**
🌬	**Windy**		

This is a weather map.
The map key shows how
to read the map. Point to
the sunny places.

Making Maps

People make maps to
help others find places.
A map key helps everyone
read the map.

What kind of map will
you make? How will a
map key help?

Words You Know

map key

pictures

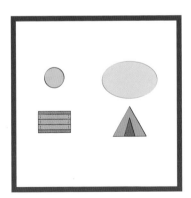

shapes

weather map

TRY IT!

Look at this map
of zoo trails. Where
is the bear? Can
you find the parrot?
Follow the forest path.
What animals do you
see on the path?

Visit this Scholastic Web site for
more information on map keys:
www.factsfornow.scholastic.com
Enter the keywords **Map Keys**

MAP KEY

bear

monkey

parrot

squirrel

forest path

jungle trail

Index

About the Author

Rebecca Olien is a teacher and author of more than 50 books for educators and children. You can often find her studying maps to find new places to go.